A Dog Called Buddha

A Dog Called

Buddha

Steve Jamison

Published by Blue Poppy Publishing
Edited by Sarah Dawes
Cover design by Oliver Tooley

ISBN: 978-1-911438-41-0
FIRST EDITION
Limited print run 100 copies

Chapter One

The setting sun

No dogs barking. Silence in the valley, not a warbler or a cicada. Two days now of silence and stillness in this gap between the worlds.

A podengo came by just now, a young one, cunning-hungry and wild. He had a short-legged black friend with him and I called them over quietly to visit, to have a cool drink, but they ran off into the forest, their fear overcoming hunger.

It's changing now, every moment; the sun is deeper below the hills and a goat's bell is sounding in the woods just above Carlos' house. Now I'm hearing another bell much closer and looking down from where I'm sitting I can see a goat under one of the fig trees. It's not the little black and white one who always manages to get in by climbing on the roof of my log store; this one is altogether a different kettle of *poissons*, a much larger person, older and more experienced, far more circumspect. I like him but this feeling isn't at all mutual, but then I doubt he likes anyone.

They all came in here this afternoon after I'd left the gate open and when I got back most of them were running around under the trees eating the flowers, but he had stayed outside, keeping an eye on them and to see if I was going to be a nuisance and ask them to leave. He's worked out very quickly I don't harm animals, which in his perspective makes me a pussy. He's an unreconstructed goat.

As I came back in, he eyeballed me and fixed me with his perfect, 'leave them alone; you know I don't like you,' stare and now he's come back, checking to see if they can all come in and feast on the fruit and flowers. Up here, in the foothills of the mountains, orchids,

1

magnolias, azaleas, sunflowers and herbs are scattered amongst the olive groves, and the goats eat most of them. So I'm getting down from up here on this terrace and I hope he'll move when I do, back to the herd and the woods.

The sun has set; it's time to go inside, light a fire and a few candles. The silence is greater somehow. I can feel the forest creatures of the night slowly stir. It will soon be their time.

Morning

It's still early and the cloud is all around. Everything is completely still; there is no sound beyond the moisture of the cloud falling onto the leaves like a sip of water to a parched tongue. I'm sitting between a fig tree and an olive, on a wall of river stones, so my feet are off the ground. I want to move, stand on the earth beneath the trees, root down and just be in this stillness. Some birds have begun to come out of the forest behind, a warbler is just in front of me and a blackbird's song cracks the air. I move and stand beneath the trees, noticing the coolness of the earth and letting go. I follow my breath, only this breath and this moment.

Lucy

She has somehow survived. She can hardly walk, just a few paces, and her eyes are all glazed over. She's looking at me though, at least she's not blind. It's a look of curiosity and recognition and behind her eyes a light is shining out of the dark.

There is no sound. It's one of those moments of deep stillness and silence here at Cha, not even a warbler or other sign of life from the forest or a distant village, not a cockerel, no dogs barking, nada. This was her silence, her solitude for so long, chained up alone in a shed for a year and fed just once or twice a week. She had to share that with the rats. She was covered with fleas and raw with mange, with patches of her own shit stuck to her. She is free now and although she can hardly walk she goes a few steps into the sunlight to lie down in the shade of the avocado, her favourite spot. I scratch her belly for her, she rolls over in a perfect moment for both of us. Did I free her or did she free me?

How it happened is a small story and it's a little thing to free just one dog from a hellhole, but this is her story.

I'd read a long time ago in the Upanishads there's a place within us all that we should get to know, to journey there, and even I realized that somewhere in the beautiful writing was a map showing how to get there, if only I had eyes to see it, to find a way. In the end Lucy showed me and this moment of stillness, up here in the foothills of the mountains, was just a few days after the beginning of our journey together.

The sound of the river

The cloud is below me now with the blue mountain sky above. Nothing is happening: everything is happening. The river has shrunk in this endless summer and its stones gawp like skulls in the dark shallows near the banks. There's no sound like before when it tumbled over them, washed them and shaped them. The sound of the river has always been here but now there is a space to be filled.

The fire

The smoke is black and dense, covering most of the sky above the valley. A solitary buzzard is soaring above, but the songbirds have flown. A wind has come up, mainly from the south, and the core of the fire is south west so it's not good, the wind will drive it.

This fire started as they always do, a trail of grey and black pluming into the blue, a distant vague shape and common enough here in the heat and months of no rain. It's growing faster than usual though, and the village siren has just sounded a warning, which happens every Sunday at 1:00 pm to test it. Lucy and I share our house with three other dogs. Two of them, a galgo and podengo, also rescues with stories, both howl like wolves at the siren and they carry on until it

3

stops. Today is Sunday but it's not 1:00 pm, it's much earlier. I'm guessing and hoping that by now the *bombeiros* will be there on the ground close to the flames and fighting them.

This fire is big though. The eucalyptus trees here in the forest burn well, good firewood in the winter, but this autumn feels like summer and the scent from the blossom on the lemon tree is like a second spring, delicate and intoxicating. Elsewhere though the forest leaves are dry and deadly. Down in the valley the dogs are disturbed, barking at more sirens, and here the galgo and podengo are still howling like wolves. The smoke is dense and black. Now more planes have arrived, glinting red and orange in the fire and the sun.

Carlos has turned up on the terrace below with all his goats and some sheep. He's standing in the middle of them, looking up. The dogs hate the goats and have gone down to the gate barking at them and Carlos, who manages a, "*mais tarde,*" see you later, as he moves the goats further up the hill. He's getting ready, moving them away from the fire, but if it comes down the hill and crosses the river we'll all be in trouble.

The planes have suddenly stopped flying over, it's odd. A solitary helicopter is zigzagging over the distant foothills of the Serra, away from us, but there's nothing else now apart from the sirens. It should mean the fire is under control and the planes have gone back, but it doesn't look like it. The flames are showing themselves now, red and yellow monsters rising up out of the smoke, swirling in the wind that is feeding them and driving them on to move across the hilltops and spread down into the valley towards us. They swallow up a house on the hill, consume it then rise up and fan out to cover the sun and the grey metal sky as it bends in the heat. They will reach us in an hour or so, it's difficult to be more exact, it could be a bit more or a bit less, but they'll come. The river won't stop them now, nothing will.

Last time a wildfire was this close to where I was living we were evacuated, no questions, just get what you need and get out. We went back two days later and the house had survived but nothing else. Two months after that the rains came and brought mudslides. It's already

October here and the rain will arrive soon. I remember what mudslides are like before I come back to the present and begin to put a few things into my truck. We drove down here in it and most of what we might need is already there, food for the dogs, bedding for them, water and so on. I turn on all the sprinklers we have and soak the trees, the ground, and the walls of the house as much as possible. There's a lot of timber in the building: wood and river stones go well together.

A smaller patch of red and yellow is in front of the main fire, like a pathfinder jumping ahead and lighting the bush; it's coming this way and I'm going down the hill to speak to Carlos to see how he is and what he's going to do.

"*Isto e mau*," this is bad, he says. He points to another ball of red and black, heading up the valley, which I hadn't seen from my place; it's creating a pincer movement and we look at each other in silence. The word fireball sinks in. He's staying he says, dowsing down the house. I tell him I'm going to leave soon, and we understand each other.

It's dark now, about an hour later. I'm up on the terrace and it's easier to see the flames from here, towering way above the black treeline. There are loud explosions on the edge of the town just up the road and beneath this is the sound of trees crashing as timber is falling all around onto the forest floor, burning to a cinder below. What of the forest creatures: the mice and squirrels, the bats and the beetles, everyone who lives there?

Some sounds, though, have gone and it's eerie. There are no sirens from the fire trucks; it's as if they've left. If so the fire must be too big and we're alone. I don't mind that; they will have done all they can.

So, it's time to leave, to say goodbye to Cha, gather in Lucy and the others, and try to find a safe place.

This fire is late; it belongs to the summer heat. Autumn here is most often a gentle affair when the sun still shines, the warblers stay around, some cicadas persist and a breeze whispers through the tree-tops.

When the rain comes, as it usually has by now, it's a new beginning. Shocking at first, the strength, the cold, and the way it becomes a small river pouring into the ravines. The forest trees and shrubs have been dried and mummified by the endless summer, and with the rain their scent explodes into an intoxicating perfume of rosemary, pine, and eucalyptus. Patches of sunlight reflect on the white walls of the hillside houses in the distance, the low cloud is darker and drifts below the mountains to hang like a thin veil over the valleys below. The church bell tolls, stillness is all around and it opens the spirit. The rain stops as quickly. A patch of blue appears above the pines, the thin sun is filtered by the oak and cork trees into silver threads that glisten on the pools of water and stones beneath them.

That is what happens but, without rain, the forest has been laid out to dry in the months of endless sun, just waiting to burn.

The way out is blocked, trees that have crashed and burned are lying across it while a few people from the village are scurrying past them back to their families. Just across the river, a stone's throw, the flames tower ten or twenty metres above the roofs of the houses. The second head of the fire will sweep over the hills behind, driven by the wind and flaring up, it will reach where we are to carry on past us into the forest behind. It's the bushfire equivalent of a perfect storm.

There is another road. It may or may not be blocked. We could get to it but if it is blocked the chance of getting back will be small. Trees line the roads here: pine, eucalyptus, oak and cork, offspring of random seeds that have found homes on the steep hillsides. Some hang at forty-five degrees over the edge of the road, and everywhere trees are burning and crashing down. They have deep roots but if some burn and do fall across the road there will be no way back. If we stay the risk is plain to see, the house is surrounded by the forest and will probably burn.

The dogs

When Lucy was freed, she came to live with the other dogs here. The podengo was picked up in the south and locked in the council pound for years. Not dangerous, he had a stay of execution. He was a complex character with strange habits and no one wanted him. He always urinated on his food bowl after he'd finished eating, wouldn't go through doorways unless they were fully open, he was a loner, snappy with others. Trust was a foreign land to him.

When he came here, if he got the chance he ran off on thieving excursions to the villages, the rubbish bins a favourite, a day and a night then he'd come back and I'd find him curled up on a terrace. A good moment.

He's been given a name, *Senhor Raposa*, Mr Fox; along with the complexes he is cunning, highly intelligent and looks remarkably like one.

The galgo was found starving in Lisbon. His name is Jimbo. Galgos here are either hunting tools or used for racing. If they no longer serve they are disposed of and this happens in very large numbers. Across the border in Spain they are sometimes called the piano dog, hung on wires to die and their feet make a noise on the ground as they hang. Their nature is gentle and loving.

Then there's a whippet, an even more accomplished thief than Fox. She opened handbags, cupboards, went into trouser pockets and had a catlike ability to jump straight up onto kitchen worktops to help herself. She ran off, with or without Fox, and had to be reclaimed from restaurant kitchens or car owners when she had jumped through an open window to root around. She's called Weasel and is the head of the pack. They fit well together: outsiders, we get on.

They're anxious now and they want to know what we're going to do. They've seen the truck being loaded with food, water, bedding and tools as the fire grew.

The road out

The second road out is surrounded on both sides by the fire, but it's not yet up to the tarmac. The wind is behind it; our direction of travel is the same and we could meet as the road twists and bends through the foothills. These fires can jump, so a new head can start and trap your escape. If that happens I hope to be able to turn back and we'll have to take our chances at the house. Evacuating now is probably the lesser of the two evils, so the plan is to take this road and snake round behind the flames, south of the black plume of smoke where it started about ten kilometres away.

We'll probably need more water. There's fuel, food, shelter in the truck, and about five litres but I was short on containers, it's very hot and we could use some more. I know of a village a few kilometres on, it's in the path of the fire but safe for now, and we drive until stopping there at a small garage where people are gathered, waiting. The garage should have some bottled water to sell, but when I ask they say there isn't any, they've sold out. I stay for a moment, chatting about the fire and where we've come from, then someone goes over to his house, brings over five litres and gives it to me. He won't accept any money and says buy him a beer next time I'm passing. A small act of kindness, often all we need.

We're up in the hills looking down into the valley. Most of the village below should be safe; the river runs through it and there is clear space either side of the buildings. We could turn around, or stay here and take our chances with the water giver, but turning back doesn't feel right and it would be a bit tricky to manage these dogs for a long time in a random group of people, most of whom will be afraid of them, so we carry on.

I listen in to the truck, an old Land Rover. We have form. Now would be a bad time for a breakdown or puncture and I breathe in through my nose, down through my chest and into my belly. It's calming and helps me focus.

Looking into the valley there is only the fire, dark red and orange, burning against the black sky. Where is safe? I can see the golden lights of a village a long way off in the distance and from here it looks as if it's right in the path of the flames. Still, this road is a way behind the fire, although it could still swing back round, with a change of wind direction, or jump. I'll have to hope and pray that it doesn't do that. We're up high now, heading towards the space behind the flames, and although the sky is still black I can see the stars behind the heavy veil of smoke.

What brings us to a certain place at a certain time? A seemingly random collection of events? Choices made? Fate, karma?

One choice made was to get Lucy out of the hell she was in. That was the final trigger, to come back and get her out, but like all triggers it was already there, just waiting.

She's next to me in the passenger seat, her first time in any vehicle for sure, and she's sitting quietly. Weasel is in the footwell, her spot, Fox is curled up in the back and Jimbo is restless, fidgeting and moving around, breathing down my neck.

It's usual here for the roads to be empty, just a tractor or pickup, a small car scurrying along, but now the sense of emptiness is deep and there is no life, all the creatures have left. I'm stopping to let the dogs drink some water, the heat is intense and more so with five bodies in this metal box. The forest here is quieter and the noise of the fire distant as we pull over.

Lucy can walk a little now, a few steps, but most of the time I'm her legs. I've got her out of the front, holding her in my arms, and Weasel has joined us from her spot in the footwell. Fox has the skill of becoming invisible and disappearing into the bush, and he won't come back unless and until he wants to. This is not the time or place. Galgos run fast like greyhounds and Jimbo would like to do that now into this forest; Fox will transmit how and when to slip past like a shadow. They have form. I have leads.

It's better now, back in the truck, another journey. Three of us have travelled thousands of miles together; Lucy and I began our journey the day her chains were cut, when I thought our trip to the vets was likely to be our first and last. They were quiet, told me later they had never seen a dog that looked in such a bad state. That was after I'd smartened her up for her visit, given her a wash in warm water, some time in the sun when we sat together and she had a cool fresh drink, then a meal she didn't have to share with the rats.

That was two months ago. Nothing sinister showed in the bloods or x-rays and although she still can't walk more than a few metres it's partly because her back legs don't align anymore, like a dysplasia. Her life force is very strong with an extraordinary will to live I've never come across before. She walks and when she stops I carry her. She likes it, a good arrangement.

The black space behind the flames is getting closer. We're going down into a valley, the hills behind are clear and will give a bearing on where the fire is heading. I can't get a sense of the wind direction down here, just the emptiness, but I can see some stars now above the hills. I'm reminded we're not really in control of our lives, we make choices that create the illusion that we are. We're on this road, beneath the stars; where did it begin and where does it end? What are we doing here? What is the purpose of this journey?

As well as the emptiness it's very dark in this valley; there's no light glowing from the fire or distant villages and no sense of life.

The road is beginning to take us up again, a gentle climb at first but getting steeper, a cliff edge on one side now and the rock face on the other, with a view from the cliff side across miles of open country glowing red and amber against the sky. There's a dirt track away from the edge on the other side and we take it, we need a place to camp and the fire is a long way off. The track leads us deep into the forest and I open up the windows to breath in the scent of pine, eucalyptus, rosemary and wild honeysuckle, heaven on earth. We can camp here, it's a clear spot.

Chapter Two

"There is the path of night and smoke, the path of the moon's dark fortnight and the six months' journey of the sun to the south: the yogi who takes this path will reach the lunar light: this path leads back to human birth, at last."

The Bhagavad Gita

It's autumn, exactly to the day in the middle of the moon's passage, the beginning of the sun's six-month journey to the south and my actions have brought me here. Karma. The night and smoke that the Bhagavad Gita is talking about is the soul's journey after death, and if this where I'm heading now, I'm not ready.

"There is the path of light, of fire and day, the path of the moon's bright fortnight and the six months' journey of the sun to the north: the knower of Brahman who takes this path goes to Brahman, he does not return."

That sounds a lot better. I think it's saying our souls can exist in a kind of endless summer of divine ground and don't have to go through another incarnation. Whether you believe in re-incarnation or not, it's way better than the alternative, this path of night and smoke. I must have got it badly wrong.

In the Bhagavad Gita, Krishna tells Arjuna how we can move to a better place through yoga, even the likes of me. The first step is for Arjuna to accept responsibility for where he is. The second is that he needs to act because he faces battle on the fields of Kurukshetra, a metaphor for life. It's a battle which we all have to meet and we can't run and hide from it.

I came here to get Lucy out. Not a difficult choice, but more difficult to do, at least for me. One other person had tried to rescue her before and met so much resistance she gave up. In the end, with help from my friend and one-time fixer Fernando, I bought the semi-derelict house she was supposed to be guarding, paying about the same as for an average second-hand car here. Worry about the money and the building later, just get her out.

So now the money's gone, the building's probably going to burn and I'm on this road in the middle of this fire in the middle of nowhere. For now I'd better make sure we make it through this path of 'night and smoke'. As far as accepting responsibility goes, that bit of the Gita, I'd do it all again. My aim was clear and never mind the road to hell being paved with good intentions, all it takes for evil to continue is for us to do nothing.

A few months ago more than sixty people died just across the mountain from where we are; they'd evacuated but were burned in their cars as the fire swept across the road. The advice is to stay put, douse everything down, and if it's an evacuation case the *bombeiros* will come and find you. The flames, though, can travel so fast and become so huge this doesn't always work and you have to get out or burn. The fires in July were the worst since the 1960s. Why again now, much bigger and far worse, just a few months later? Climate change is a big factor of course, but also here mismanagement and the shift from native oaks to pine and eucalyptus play a part in this lethal mix. In the last century Salazar's dictatorship planted huge swathes of eucalyptus trees in this central part of the country, to be used for paper, industrializing nature; the eucalyptus began to replace all the other trees and is full of oil that the flames adore. The diversity went and so did a lot of the people, leaving the countryside untended and much of it with no identified ownership and so uncared for. The bush grows year after year, waiting for a lightning strike, an electrical fault somewhere, a careless or deliberate match.

I have to tether the dogs or they'll run into the forest. We begin to find our sleeping places for the night, surrounded mainly by pine and eucalyptus, but the scent of the honeysuckle is a great comfort. I've often slept with the dogs: they move around in the night, swap beds, dream and growl sometimes or wake up and bark at something. We're talking now, they're settling, and it's me who's unsettled.

Fires are fickle. For now it's heading northwest but it's out of control and menacing. I don't want to make a mistake; I'm responsible for the dogs and only a fool wouldn't feel edgy about their own safety as well. If we interfere with the path of another, as I've done with the dogs, it's the same as the shamanic example of picking up a snail who was crossing the road: the action has responsibility attached to it. The Gita says we also have to deal with the inaction of not picking it up.

The scent of the honeysuckle is everywhere and I want to find it. I put Lucy back on her seat in the truck and take the others into the woods, following my nose to a cluster of ferns and a small *modregno* tree where the honeysuckle has spread all around to almost reach a nearby pine. I stand for a few minutes, breathe it all in and we head back to bed down in the truck. It's familiar, there are no ants and it provides a thin but definite barrier between Fox and the forest. He would be cunning enough to wait before slipping his collar and disappearing into the shadows beneath these tall pines.

It's cramped though. Stretched out, Jimbo is about the same length as me, nearly six feet, and he won't curl up. Fortunately Weasel and Lucy fit in the front and, once Fox accepts there'll be no vanishing acts, he settles down by me, curls up and crosses his white paws.

I won't be able to sleep, not for a while at least, and I'm going to do a yoga nidra, which is a way of deeply relaxing. It is wide-ranging, and it's better to set our intention before we begin. You can use it if you need a break and may only have half an hour or so, and afterwards it lets us carry on, feeling much better and refreshed. It can also be used to develop areas of consciousness which we don't normally inhabit. You direct your mind to specific parts of the body moving in rotation, usually from right to left, including individual fingers and toes, the right eye, left eye and so on. I begin with my right toe.

Vasana

I'm awake, refreshed after yoga nidra. With the window open and scent of the forest it feels like a heavenly realm up here beneath the moon and stars, untouched by the hell below, but although refreshed I feel very disturbed. A lot of creatures won't survive; livestock and domestic animals will somehow have to fend for themselves and human beings will die. It revives a memory I carry of animals and humans I was unable to save. Yogic philosophy accepts such memories, that present to us like imprints we can't explain, as soul memories we bring into our lives. They are called vasanas, and can inhabit our psychic landscape like a perfume, a scent that remains in the room after the person wearing it has left. There are other ways of looking at them, the collective unconscious or a kind of ancestral coding for example, and if possible we need to see where they fit in for us if one crops up. At least one Tibetan yogi says he has complete knowledge of all his past incarnations for example. Without becoming self-absorbed it's common sense to have an idea of our inner landscape.

One vasana bothered me for a long time; it came up as I was quietly minding my own business and walking with my collie dog through heavy mud and rain in the early morning of an English winter. It was as if I suddenly slipped through time and space and I was shocked to hear a voice say, "When you get back sir, have a drink for me." I looked, there was no one around and at the same time I felt transported to a battlefield, with a searing pain in my right ankle. It was raining, the mud was like slurry and the stench of death overwhelming. It only lasted briefly but was very intense and disquietingly familiar. I carried on walking with my collie, glad to be exactly where I was. That night I had a vivid dream where I was back on the battlefield, the same familiar stench was all around and I was responsible for men who were no more than boys. My right foot had been severed at the ankle and I was helped up onto a cart of wounded. Their bandages were oily rags, bits of torn shirt, paper with string or rope round it, and the cart was a mess of defecation, urine, pus, of visible sinews and flesh hanging from bones: wounds so awful I would have rather been dead than have to bear them. It was still raining and we had to cross the deep mud on timber boards where men kept falling off into the slurry, exhausted horses stumbled and fell, but we had to press on and leave them all or be blown to pieces by the enemy's artillery.

I thought of a possible ancestral connection to the strange episode on the walk and this awful dream. I had three great-uncles who met their deaths at the Somme and my father was named after each one of them, but I couldn't see how such memories would be directly transmitted down through two generations since my uncles died before ever returning home.

So far this fire has kept to its path. It has spread up the hillsides and is heading northeast. It will be fickle in whom and what it burns though; in the wildfires I've been in before I remember how some houses are left untouched while others close to them become jagged skeletons, the smoke still rising from them and the nearby fire holes days later. The fire doesn't care if Senhora so-and-so is very nice and Senhor so-and-so really isn't, you can get this situation where one neighbour's house has burnt and they're left with nothing while the other is untouched.

Cha is on a hillside to the north-east of where we are and right in the path of the flames. A smaller fire two years ago came within twenty feet of the house. The flames of these fires often reach beyond the tree tops and the pines and eucalyptus here can be thirty metres high or more, so the flames are often over a hundred feet when they're coming your way. The tallest tree in Europe is a eucalyptus in Valle de Canas, seventy-three metres high and about an hour's drive from where we are now. The last fire here devastated the hills for miles around and the local word was that would be it for years. Folklore, experience handed down over generations, before the planet warmed up, before the ice began to melt.

I slept eventually and a robin has woken me up. I listen to it for a while before getting out of the truck to look for it in the nearby oak.

15

Lucy has got out as well and is slowly zigzagging towards the forest, falling over but struggling to her feet again. I've never seen her walk more than a few paces and she's managed about twenty. I'd left a small gap when I got out to avoid any noise, so the robin and any other birds might stay, and I was still keeping an eye on her when all the other dogs jumped over the front seat and got out too, running around in different places. They're a rabble. I let this chaos happen for a short while and then dig out their food bowls so they'll come running for breakfast while I go to fetch Lucy and carry her back for hers. She's lying down and knows I'm on my way.

Tea, black, with soya milk mixed with a little honey in a tin mug, water boiled on the small gas stove in a pan in the back of the truck – very careful with this because of the forest floor as well as flames from the stove and boiling water around the dogs. The tea with honey is mingling with the scent of the honeysuckle as it opens to the early morning sun and I'm drinking in all of it.

It's time for some yoga, to really wake up. We do it every morning together and Lucy likes to come and sit on the mat so with standing postures I have to adjust a bit to fit round her. They are warming, grounding and allow my body to open more to the sitting ones. She stays for them too, stares at me the whole time and her eyes light my spirit.

We have to go back, to find out if we still have a home, and as the road descends into the valley the scent of the pine and rosemary is replaced by acrid smoke; it's dark, empty and unsettling. We don't get very far, two *bombeiros* by the roadside pull us over, say the road is blocked and we have to go back. I ask where they're from. It's Lisbon, hundreds of miles away; they don't know the hills and valleys and are having to rely on Google maps on their tablets. Their energy is low, deflated, and they know they've lost this battle.

It doesn't feel good to turn back, but we head back up the hill to the forest and take the same track to our camp and I somewhat randomly drive on a little way to another clearing. We all feel restless. A normal day would see the dogs out running in the hills near Cha, and Lucy lying in the sun or finding her way back to the shade beneath the avocado tree. Now we'll have to settle here and wait.

Agni

The yogic word for fire is agni, also the word for fire in Hindi, from the Sanskrit. In both, agni has the mystical power to transform, an energy that literally enlightens us. In yoga this transformative energy is linked to the kundalini energy and agni clears the way for the energy to be released. Just as oxygen is a vital component to fire, so the breath and how we breathe is vital to fully release the energy.

Enough waiting here though, I'm going to try and get back to Cha, find another way, head north and see if we can loop back round. It will mean heading off up a small track I noticed before we got to the *bombeiros* and it might take us to a road which is clear.

The track is narrow. We've turned off before the roadblock and I could see from above the valley the main fire was heading north and we're following it but a little to the east. Some ash is falling and if it gets thicker I'm turning round; there could be sparks that ignite the forest behind us. The fire a few years ago covered the house with ash and during the days of cleaning that followed I was thinking it wouldn't happen again for years. That was a big fire, but this one is altogether something different, the wind from the hurricane driving it across millions of hectares just waiting to ignite.

These wildfires are part of an underlying process. Climate change has been happening for a long time now and is a major part of all this but the foothills here increase the intensity and speed of the flames. Now the land is densely planted with eucalyptus and they spread quickly from the buds buried deep in their bark to suck water from the soil, drying out the ecosystem. Planting them on an industrial scale was going to end like this and allowing them to spread up to the roadside would sooner or later create the death trap that happened this summer just across the mountain.

The ash is getting thicker but I'm carrying on for a while longer to climb uphill again and see more. It's the usual snaking up around the twists and turns of these tracks, looking down onto the occasional small village nestling into the slopes, just a field or two before the edge of the forest. More fields and less forest would help control the fire risk but people have left these villages for the towns and cities or to work abroad so there are fewer people to take care of the land and large areas are left unattended. A farming cooperative near Cha rents out their land for eucalyptus, which is sold to the paper companies. Now it's all burning but they'll replant more and hope they can harvest it before the next fire. The cycle is obvious; the question is how to break it, what will it take to move out of this monoculture. Even if that happens, climate change is here and these fires are now devastating large areas of every continent on our planet.

We're fortunate: the track picks up the road and we should be able to head a bit further north-east and loop back round towards Cha. I slow down to walking pace and open the window, I can smell the fire but can't hear it. Good. We carry on to the top of another hill where smoke is curling up from smouldering eucalyptus trees. There are holes around them and small flames, but there is nothing left to burn now. For as far as I can see I'm looking down onto a smoking desert. Thousands of hectares, black trees, black earth, pockets of fire still burning red and orange in the morning sun. There is no sound, no sign of life, not even a siren in the distance, the battle was lost some time ago and there are no witnesses here to the trail of devastation, they've all fled. Some houses are burnt out. The roofs have gone, the walls are jagged and broken, nothing remains of them. We go on down the hill and, if we can keep going, the road should eventually loop back to Cha but it won't be straightforward. Telephone poles are uprooted with their wires twisted and tangled up on the road, electricity cables are hanging down, some have landed on nearby trees and others are spread across the tarmac. I'm wondering again about all the wildlife caught up in this disaster.

Chapter Three

We all suffer to some degree here on Earth. Yoga calls this dukkha. A lot of people simply need some clean water to drink, shelter, and some food in their bellies. If we have that already, it's a good start.

When I was in Africa we spent the whole day around water. Get up in the morning, walk to the well, fetch the water, drink some, and grind the maize to eat later. Drink some more water, eat a few cola nuts, cook some rice, wash in the water we'd cooked in and live through another day. At night the whole village became a magical realm where the children dressed up in dark green silken clothes and put on cheap jewellery, which shone like diamonds in the moonlight. We lit a fire and the stars lit the sky, some of the children played beautiful music on *koras*, small harps, and there was drumming deep into the night as one by one we went back to our mud huts to sleep. They had nothing and gave me everything.

Juju

"See that man? He's a lion man, he changes into a lion. You need to wear this now, this is good juju, it will protect you." I stared into the eyes of the speaker, a youngish man; we hardly knew each other beyond occasionally sharing food and water, trips to the well and a smile as we passed. He handed me a leather amulet to wear on my wrist and I put it on. We were in a bar, part of a shop which stocked a collection of random things, sold beer and soft drinks. The lion man was sitting at the other end with a few people and looked harmless enough to me. I realized later he was a local shaman and the amulet wasn't to protect me from him but to ward off bad energy generally.

There was also the vague scent of marijuana in the bar although no one was visibly smoking. I'd come across it before, in a hut next door to mine, when I was spending some time in the town and found a place to stay which was cheap and where no one seemed to bother anyone else. One afternoon I was passing by their door which was wide open, they were sitting around inside and I could smell the grass they must have just been smoking. They smiled and beckoned me to go inside, I smiled back and went in. They were quiet, closed the door and handed me a bible.

"Open it man, where's it at?" one of them said, a big guy whose whole face was a smile. It was the New Testament of John.

"Ah, John is good," the big man said, and handed me a bag of brownish grass which had probably come up on a boat from Ghana. The local weed was twiggy and green.

"Take a page an' roll a spliff man!" he said, and this town bible group sat patiently while I took a single page out and rolled a joint. I had a couple of tokes and then passed it on. "No man, that's yours, we all make our own." So I smoked the whole page and inhaled the words fully and deeply.

I still had the amulet on a few days later when the heat and moonlight took me to my old Honda bike for a ride out along the dirt track into the bush. I'd smoked more of the grass which I was now doing regularly along with the other local habit of chewing cola nuts. It was clear and bright and I think I was looking up at the stars on the horizon when I hit a bump in the road. It was big and must have been in the shadow of something. As I came off I saw the shadow's mother, a baobab tree, looming like a mountain as I flew towards it.

I came round beneath the tree, looking up through its bare branches to the stars. There was no pain, just a deep sense of calm. I felt around my body, no broken bones, no blood, still no pain, and not even a scratch on my bare arms and head. I lay there for a short while staring up at all the stars and then got up. My bike was on its side in the savannah so I picked it up, kick-started it and carried on. Some years later I read that the baobab tree is also called the tree of life.

Two days later it was Christmas Day. For the village it was another day of fetching water and grinding the maize. It was hot and dry, and I was going to spend some time alone in the bush outside the compound to be with nature and ingest a local psychoactive plant. Africa is full of medicinal plants, and they're used for every illness from snakebites to heart disease, diabetes, blood pressure issues, arthritic conditions and so on, often with very good results. It's the function of the local doctor to diagnose and administer. These doctors were called witch doctors by the whites, but on the whole were mainly trained and experienced shamans with an extensive knowledge of plants, the physical and non-physical realms, and instead of an exchange of knowledge and wisdom we forced on them a diet of Little Bo Peep and Humpty Dumpty.

The plants vary in strength and effect and I didn't know what I was taking, other than it was psychotropic and the locals called it *kubi jarra*, cures everything. I was told it could also make you go blind, a risk I wouldn't take now but did then. I skipped breakfast, a precaution against vomiting, mixed up the brown powder in a bowl and drank it all down. About fifteen minutes later I walked to a quiet place in the bush where there were some rocks. A good spot.

It was hot. The sun was up, I felt into the heat all around creating stillness where nothing really stirs unless it needs to, like a snake in the grass. I sat on a large rock, felt its heat penetrating my body and as I went to lie down on it heard a loud noise, a scrunching of things rubbing together that was getting louder and coming my way. I sat up again but couldn't see anything. At the same time I had a sense of watching myself sitting on the rock. I stared into the space where the noise seemed to be coming from, past the rocks into the bush, and some eyes stared back at me, large pools of suffering below enormous horns and a skull covered with a thin layer of brown hair. He looked away and carried on his path, a skeletal body of ribs sticking out beneath skin stretched like a drum over his bones. He was followed by another, and flies, a lot of flies. It was a small herd of bullocks who would be slaughtered and eaten: tough sinewy meat from these males who didn't produce milk and whose fate was sealed from birth. Then I was detached again and looking down on myself sitting on the rock before I was back in my body. I felt the heat, the dryness of everything, and wondered if the bullocks were real or imaginary. I'd lost touch with any sense of time and place.

The sun got higher and I kept looking down on myself sitting there on the rock and then being in my body again, waiting for something to happen, and during one of these moments I got up off the rock and began walking in what I hoped was the direction of the village, although I didn't have a clue which way to go. I was completely disorientated and went very slowly, feeling into the heat which was a comfort.

I walked straight back to the village, surprised at how easy it was to find my way, how close it had been. I headed to my hut, drank some water, ate some peanuts, lay down on my bed and closed my eyes. There were visions of lions, snakes, and African faces staring at me, men who held the snakes in their hands and beckoned me. I lost all sense of time and place again, then heard drumming in the village and got up.

People were getting ready for the evening, preparing the fire, and some children played nearby with small sticks of brushwood used for kindling. Women boiled the rice using up the last clean water and it felt good and grounded me.

The sensations of the *kubi jarra* had waned and I returned to a sense of time and place, of knowing where I was, but the experience raised questions about the episodes when I was looking down on my own body. Later I read up what I could about this. The information broadly fell into two camps: the neurological and psychological, or paranormal. The first camp named the experience self-bilocation with a lot of different explanations. The paranormal camp saw it as the spirit leaving the body, lining up with the shamanic, which felt more in line with my own experience. These days I see it also aligns with yogic cosmology, where the physical, astral, and causal body link to corresponding layers of energy, the koshas. There are five koshas, which are made up of the physical energy sheath through to the most subtle, which is where an out-of-body experience can take place. We can connect to the koshas in yoga practice, they flow in and around us and link to our energy centres.

After the *kubi jarra* I felt cleansed and that it was the right place to be right where I was, to feel the warmth, smell the savannah and the food cooking. I was very hungry.

The Yoga Sutras

The great thing about *The Yoga Sutras* is that Patanjali is saying that everything we experience has relevance, contrasting with nearly every religion, for example, where the main relevance is a particular Godhead. Yoga opens a way where we ourselves can directly experience something different and it doesn't depend on anything or anyone other than ourselves. It is a path to stillness and the yoga sutras are a guide, a tapestry of threads drawing the Vedas, Upanishads and the Bhagavad Gita together into a way they can begin to help us in our daily lives with great benefit, especially if we link them to a practice.

The Upanishads are the poetry of the spirit; the Bhagavad Gita is the testament of the teachings of Krishna. Each of these needs to be read and re-read a little bit at a time as they are very dense. The sutras are a map of yoga, and even absorbing just a little has been a great help to me.

The only way we can benefit from the sutras is by practice, not just the asanas, the postures, but the other seven limbs of yoga. Patanjali describes these in Sadhana Pada, the second part of the sutras, where he introduces the limbs or parts of yoga: yama, niyama, asana, pranayama, pratyahara, dharana, dhyana, and samadhi. They all interlink and in our practice can develop together. Anyone of us can begin a practice if we can breathe. Yoga isn't about how bendy we are, it's an inner journey. You could start yoga lying in bed. In fact it's a good way to start, because you won't be trying to push yourself into a place that your body isn't ready for yet like I did for about twenty years. Beginning with the breath is essential and we can do that lying down.

Asana (postures) and Pranayama (the breath) really need to form the basis of our practice, along with trying to bring the yamas and niyamas into our daily lives; even absorbing and practising a little bit of them can be very beneficial. TKV Desikachar says this in his beautifully understated but authoritative way: yoga moves us to a better place.

Postures provide a way in and by doing a little each day we can notice an improvement. People sometimes struggle with the everyday aspect of practice, and one way round this is to do one or two postures that you like doing or can do easily, perhaps gently rotating your arms and shoulders while in Tadasana (Mountain posture) and seeing if you can join the breath with the movement. If your shoulders are stiff or painful, or standing up is too much, perhaps lie down for a short while and notice your breath, see if you can develop an awareness of its natural flow, quality, the gentle rise and fall of your belly. Let it be a natural process like the rise and fall of waves on the beach. This is a beginning and already creating changes in your body, affecting the cells throughout.

The yamas deal with how we move through the world and are a code of our behaviour towards other people and other sentient beings. They are ahimsa, non-violence; aparigraha, not reaching and grabbing; asteya, not stealing; bramacharya, being contained, not spilling out; satya, telling the truth, not living in a world of deceit.

The niyamas deal with how we treat ourselves and they are saucha, keeping ourselves clean; santosa, acceptance; swadiyaya, looking at ourselves and into who we are; isvarara pranidana, acceptance of a unifying energy in the universe and acting accordingly; tapas, how we go about all this.

24

Ahimsa is so important to our presence on Earth and, practised by itself, provides us with a way out of the madness of war and damage to our planet. Gandhi-ji, a yogi initiated into the kryas by Paramahansa Yogananda, is the best-known practitioner of this yama. Typically, when questioned about some of the difficulties India was experiencing when he led the country's independence movement, Gandhi-ji said he was still learning.

I didn't know about all the limbs of yoga when I was practising postures from my book on hatha yoga decades ago. The yamas and niyamas aren't part of hatha, which is based on preparing the body so we can open to other realms of experience through physical practices that we can control, like the cleansing practices, pranayama and postures. It's not *kubi jarra* but it changes our sensory input nevertheless and keeps us healthy.

In the village the food was nearly ready, a delicious spicy stew of groundnuts with sweet potato and rice. Somehow there was always enough and it was one of the best meals for me as a vegetarian. Later on, when I found out about the industrialization of the dairy industry, the suffering it caused, and read up on how mechanized farming was a big factor in climate change, it wasn't difficult to transition to a fully plant-based diet. If the human race does evolve from meat eating and dairy consumption, it will be seen in the same light as other ways we have progressed.

We sat on the earth together eating our meal and they talked and laughed; it was a happy time and afterwards the children dressed up in their dark green clothes and played their *koras*, one of the most beautiful sounds humans have created.

As time slipped by, I found my way back to town one day and my bible group sitting in the same place. They were keen students. I was relieved the holy book wasn't brought out again with another whole page for me. These days I would feel uncomfortable tearing a page from the Bible, I wouldn't do it. Back then it felt alright; I had seen a deeply negative aspect of the church and its violent history across the world and I was happy to attend this congregation of Rastas. They were drumming, a great pastime in West Africa and something else Africans excel at. I had a guitar, went to get it from my compound and tentatively began jamming around their rhythms and singing, feeling free and at home with them. Another of their gifts was the heart energy which vibrated around them like the sun. We did this every day for some time. I had very little money and began playing a few songs in exchange for food in one of the hotels that had sprung up to cater for Scandinavians seeking winter sun and African lovers. Abba was being played very loud very often and I was just a curiosity washed up on their expensive beach.

Valley of the swallows

The road is looking a little dangerous because of the electric cables: some ahead are very low over the tarmac. The eucalyptus trees close to the roadside are still smouldering and some have fallen into the road. It should be passable, and if we get through the rest may be alright. The cables are low because the poles have fallen away to one side, burnt but not right through and their outer casing looks intact. I can't drive round them because one side is smouldering forest and the other side a steep drop into the ravine.

Stay or go, fast or slow? If I go there's a full-length roof rack on the truck which could get snagged up, so to get out of the cable mess I'll need to judge the gap pretty accurately. If I delay, the eucalyptus hanging right by the roadside might completely collapse so I reckon it's better to try to get through. I stop the truck just before the cables to have a look and realize I've pulled in directly under one I hadn't seen; it's black like everything else and I missed it. It's badly fractured and hanging right above us, so I jump back in the truck, pull away, have another quick look at the gap, accelerate and I'm sure I closed my eyes as we squeezed through. The road is still twisting round the hillsides and there are trees lying across parts of it but it looks as if we can carry on. I'm going to pull over, give the dogs some water and take a few minutes.

The Earth and everything that was living here where I'm standing is in pain and shock. All matter is energy, every stone, every leaf, nothing is separate. My friends in Africa know that intuitively and their *kora* music puts us where humans should consciously be, somewhere between the earth and sky. The reliance our culture has put in the world of things has led us down a road which is blocked and it's not the way home.

Fox wants to go. He fixes his eyes on me and nods his head, huge podengo ears erect and twitching. He nodded his head from day one around food, telling me where he wanted me to put it so he could keep watch as he ate. He doesn't like it here and is speaking for all of us.

Back on the road it should be familiar now as we're getting closer to Cha, but it's the same smouldering black void that we have been in and I don't recognize it until there is a steep descent into the valley. It bends round and levels out into what used to be a pine wood, which is now full of smoke and smouldering pockets of fire surrounding the remaining trees. I drive on; it's not far from the house, maybe eight to ten kilometres, and we have a good chance of getting there and back to our home.

I remember an evening swim in the river when I first came here about ten years ago. I was alone, the steep sides of the cliff face reflected in the deep water. I could see the shallows just a little further on, big round stones and rocks to sit on, and as I swam towards them and into the sun a kingfisher darted over my head. We're getting closer to that spot now, high up on the road that curves round the hills above the river, probably not too far from where the kingfisher would have been nesting in the bank. From here there's a clear view that once looked almost alpine, the green plain by the water spreading out to the faraway hills. Swallows gathered here, and swifts climbed to the nearby cliff tops before plummeting down almost like peregrines to the valley below, but unlike a peregrine they'd suddenly swerve into a radical manoeuvre and back again as if for fun. Sand martins lived in the cliff face and in the summer sun they all joined in a festival of light over the river.

Other festival goers gathered along its banks, in the forest and the garden at Cha, exotic creatures with exotic names. Fritillaries with slightly different markings, tortoiseshells, swallowtails, black-veined whites, holly blues, they all joined in our butterfly ball. Stag beetles came along to this garden party as well, meandering like drunks from the bathroom to the kitchen, and uninvited guests like hawkmoths found their way in and had to be shown the door for their own wellbeing.

The valley was a paradise that's just been destroyed. I need to re-focus on the road ahead and avoid the steep drop just a few feet away.

We find the truth by intuitive knowledge, the truth about who we are, and what we're doing here on this earth. Our thirst for evidence-based truth hasn't always been helpful. The shamans in Africa were clear about their worlds and how to move in and between them, good energy and bad energy. Their use of plants to open their consciousness was reflected in the use of soma juice by yogis for the same purpose, but after any initial awakening came the practice and ethical codes of behaviour. With yoga though it also works the other way round: if we do it regularly it can wake us up. It doesn't need to be veiled in any fake mysticism, endlessly mind-numbing explanations or pushing into torturous postures our bodies aren't ready for. We need to establish a practice for ourselves and do it. We embody the universe in every cell and yoga is a good way to help us experience some of this, and in this sense the practice is the guru along with the yamas and niyamas, the codes of behaviour.

It's important to do yoga every day, even if we are ill. This isn't as tough or as hard as it sounds because if we're really too sick to get out of bed we can do yoga lying down by focusing on the breath and our body. It's an opportunity to gently practise the full yogic breath for example and, if you've already some familiarity with the energy body, to engage with it. Chronic bad health like ME, which is so debilitating, can be helped with yoga but at the same time we shouldn't put stress on the body, something which applies to all of us. I spent years pushing myself into this or that posture, and what I learned from that is not to do it. The breath is key. I worked with a very good yoga teacher for years and learned a great deal more about the postures and the yoga texts, but there wasn't enough attention given to the breath and, for a long time, I was still pushing myself every day with a very demanding practice rather than be guided by the breath.

It's better to do a practice in the morning before beginning the day if at all possible. If there are children in the house or animals or babies of course you have to meet their needs. If by then you're hungry and it feels too late to practise or you have to go to work, try standing in Tadasana for a few breaths, and as you do this posture develop a sense of the breath itself moving your body. It's a subtle, important step. If you do this, you may find your arms move outwards as if by themselves and when the inhalation is complete they will be at roughly thirty to forty degrees from your trunk, the classic old school Tadasana. It will take just a few minutes and it teaches you to move from the inside and you can then begin also to direct your attention to the spine and lengthen it. If you've missed your morning practice look for a space elsewhere in the day, some standing postures outside somewhere, or when you get back home. If you focus and work closely with the breath, a lot can be done in twenty minutes. We can talk ourselves out of pretty much anything, but there's not really an excuse not to do some kind of practice.

Fox knows we're getting close to Cha and has begun to move around in the back and now Jimbo is up too. Weasel hates being in the truck and is still curled up in the footwell; Lucy is sitting quietly next to me on the front passenger seat. I'm going to have to stop and settle Fox and Jimbo, who has a bad habit of pushing into the cab between the seats and knocking my arms when I'm driving. He's very big and strong. They won't settle unless I make a point and stop to tell them. They calm down, but it won't last because we're too close and they know it; I'll have to pull over again if we don't get there soon.

I wind down the window and it lets in the acrid smell so familiar from the other fires, penetrating everything and lingering for months. We're on the road near the river in another spot and close to the track that leads up to Cha. More telegraph poles are down, some are lurching at forty-five degrees from the road and like the other ones their cables are spread across the surface along with tree branches and skinny eucalyptus trunks.

Turning into the track I can see Carlos' house is still standing, a good sign but I know that every house is different, and fires seem to choose what to take and what to leave. We're closer to the forest, which will have burnt, and the back of the house is about two metres from the pine and cork trees that hang over my roof from land that no one seems to own. To cut down cork trees here requires a special permission from the forestry commission, simple enough if you know who owns them but not so simple if you don't.

There's no sign of life: no birds, no Carlos, no little dog sunning himself on the track, no goats and nothing for them to eat now even if they survived. It's all been burnt and is still smouldering. I can see flames curling up from tree roots and fire holes as I turn the corner, slow down and park up.

I let the dogs out and we go into the garden first. It is untouched, still green and vibrant with figs on the trees and a few late pears hanging on the high branches. It's like an oasis in the black desert that surrounds it, where everything else is charred, blistered and still burning. I can't see how the garden has remained untouched, how that's possible.

I leave the dogs here and go up to the other house where Lucy was kept chained up. It's surrounded on all four sides by trees: an oak copse is directly in front of it and next to that is a line of olives and some fig trees, which are very close. I expect the trees will have burnt and the flames will have got to the roof timbers. Going up the track I pause at the corpse of a beautiful oak, black and hollowed out by the flames that still light the woodland in patches beneath a veil of smoke.

The dogs don't like being left. When this happens unexpectedly they howl. Fox always starts it then Jim. It's endless now with no breaks and, in this bitter smell, the smoke, fires and standing by this poor old oak, it sounds exactly right.

Oaks generally withstand fire better than many other trees, and although the ones in front of the house are badly burnt they don't look completely destroyed and some of them might recover. The olives have been ruined but a fig tree has somehow survived and the side of the house looks intact. The fire must have been worse on the other side though, where the eucalyptus would have blazed, spreading onto the pines then into long grass below and right up to the rear wall where Lucy was imprisoned. I can hear her now, below in the other house, barking long after the others, even Fox, have stopped. She never gave in and she never gives in now, her uncanny determination and guts so evident in how she tackles the hills and steps; an extraordinary spirit.

There's a wall at the rear of the house which has burnt. A severed water pipe is hanging down but I need to get into the courtyard to see the rest, which is exposed to the eucalyptus on the hillside behind it. The courtyard is closed off by high metal doors typical of many properties here; its lock is old, rusty and was broken but has been mended so that to open it you have to put the key in upside down and then turn it clockwise. I've forgotten that and I'm fiddling with it before I can push one of the doors back.

It was cleaned up here after getting Lucy out, when it was partly covered by a corrugated iron roof and a vine which spread at head height from one side to the other. Below that was a log pile, chicken wire and some broken agricultural tools. Empty plastic tubs, bits of food wrapping, some bones, more wire and, at the far end, Lucy's chain poked out like the Devil's tail. Around that was about a foot of dried shit where she'd had to go, chained to an area of about two metres. The first time we went in to clean it I was with three men who knew it was going to be dirty work. After about two minutes we all ran out, they took off their shirts and we were jumping up and down on the earth covered in fleas, hundreds of them; a feast where they gorged on our fresh bodies and hopped all over our skin as we stripped off in the morning sun.

There comes a point with fleas and mosquitos where you simply have to go to war. The mosquitos out here can be relentless. As the Dalai Lama said, if you think you're too small to make a difference try sleeping with a mosquito in your tent.

When we went back a few weeks later we cleared out the remains of the rubbish and more plastic mixed in with the rest of Lucy's shit dried hard in the sun. We cleaned again and hosed everywhere down so now only the vine remains, deep rooted and spreading across some wire left stretched high up over the courtyard, a rat run into the roof space. They'll have survived, will come back and find a cosy spot in the roof and walls, scrabbling around at night and being a nuisance.

I can see now that some of this house has burnt and all the surrounding land right up to its walls is charcoal black and still smouldering. The kitchen wall has gone and the pipe work running along outside it, all the fruit trees that line the bank behind and every olive tree. The house should have burnt completely: it's open with broken windows, dirty guttering full of debris, dried out wood is hanging from the ceilings inside and eucalyptus trees grow close enough for the wind to take streamers of burning bark onto the exposed roof timbers. How did it escape?

I head back to the dogs feeling blessed to be alive. I know others will not have been so fortunate.

Jimbo

The river at the gorge.

Lucy after being rescued.

The fire – first signs.

The fire – getting worse.

The fire – out of control.

Fox on the terrace.

All the dogs: Weasel, Fox, Lucy and Jimbo.

The track into the hills.

One of the dragonflies.

Chapter Four

In the Katha-Upanishad a man seeking salvation gives away all his property, which mainly consists of animals. His son Nachiketas, who is still very young and watching all this go on, asks his father if he's giving him away as well. His father doesn't answer straightaway, but then tells his son he's given him away to Death. When he heard his father say this Nachiketas thought what mattered to him most was what would happen if Death got hold of him at that very moment, so he leaves his father straightaway, on bad terms, and goes into the forest to find Death. He sits without any food or water for days until Death appears in front of him and says, "You've been sitting waiting for me and here I am. But you have sat so patiently and still, I'm going to offer you three gifts."

The first gift Nachiketas asks for is reconciliation with his father and Death grants it, saying all will be well and his father will love him as before.

The second gift he asks for is for a way to Heaven. He rightly points out to Death, "You're not there, nobody there is afraid of dying, and no one is hungry or thirsty or sad." Nachiketas continues, "You know what fire leads to Heaven; I ask that fire to be my second gift." Death gives a very full and, on the face of it, straightforward answer but not to the specific reference to fire. He tells Nachiketas that the way to Heaven is firstly to adopt a path of knowledge, meditation and practice; the second part is connected to discernment, what is evidence, inference, experience; and lastly to embrace study, concentration and renunciation. It was a mammoth undertaking but the rishis who went into the forest did it and they took sannyasa, the renunciation of worldly desire to live an ascetic life. Heaven was aligned to samadhi: not a place but a realm of consciousness.

The reference to fire by Nachiketas is a thread to how the kundalini energy can be awaked by practices involving clearing the way, as a fire, to remove obstacles on the path to heaven. This would include specific ways of breathing to unite the practitioner with the life force in themselves and the universe. Death puts this practice into the context of life as an ascetic in the forest; concentration comes before the last step of sannyasa because he is referring to practice and meditations which require full concentration. He's saying there are no short cuts.

Death makes it clear to Nachiketas that he has fulfilled the second gift and asks him what he wants for his third gift. Nachiketas says, "Some say that when we die we continue to exist and others say we don't. Can you explain this as my third gift?" Death tells him to ask for something else, but Nachiketas persists and begins to wear him down. Death offers him all sorts of things, including a really long life of endless joy and pleasure, but Nachiketas won't give up, pointing out that even a long human life is short, "So say where we go when we die." Finally Death provides an answer and begins by telling Nachiketas that there is a unified source of all life in the universe which he refers to as Spirit. He says that this also lives within us, in our hearts. He then responds to the specific question about what happens to us after death. "Some enter the womb, waiting for a moving body, some pass into unmoving things, according to deed and knowledge." So he is saying some of us are reborn and some of us become part of everything else in the universe with no re-incarnation, depending on deed, on how we have moved through the world, our actions or inaction. Knowledge here means direct experience that all life is connected.

The sutras, a tapestry woven from threads interlinking endlessly between themselves, also contain links to the Upanishads and the Bhagavad Gita, which relate to this explanation by Death. The eighth limb of samadhi is the direct experience of oneness with what the Upanishads call Spirit. We always look for evidence-based proof and physicists, biochemists and others concluding that all life is connected is a good start, but for thousands of years the rishis not only made this clear but also found a path which, if followed, could lead us to experience this for ourselves. It was important to have a pathfinder to light the way, a guru, and there was a selection process for those who wanted to join, to climb the mountains, descend into the valleys and penetrate the dark forests of their journey. Then, as now, the darkness could only be seen for what it was by shedding light on it, but first we have to go there. This is swadiyaya in the sutras: self-inquiry.

The words 'according to deed and knowledge', which Death brings up, reappear in the Bhagavad Gita. At the beginning Arjuna is faced with a huge battle but unable to engage because some of his family and friends are in the enemy's ranks. He despairs and puts down his weapons, but Krishna tells him that the hour of battle has come and he must act. Krishna seems to be inciting a battle and death here but seen as a metaphor, where he is talking about facing our demons, it works well.

Arjuna is told that strong people don't wallow in despair because, "it wins neither heaven nor earth," and Krishna tells him to, "rise up like a fire," or put some fire in his belly, so to speak. But it is also a reference to the raising of the kundalini energy and to the fire of agni, where ignition happens just below our belly and rises up through our energy body by way of the nadis.

The Upanishads, the Bhagavad Gita and the sutras are clear that humans have a nature which allows us to directly experience unity with all life on earth and in the cosmos. Our purpose is to uncover that nature and to live a life which reflects it. For the rishis, total immersion in the natural world was a keystone and relates to why many names for yogic postures are taken from animals. A high proportion of our DNA is shared with plants and animals who share the earth with us.

"This earth is the honey of all beings, and all beings the honey of this earth."

Brihadaranyaka-Upanishad

Wildfires began here about four hundred million years ago, after plants started growing. We live on a planet that burns. It's a good place for it: oxygen, vegetation, plenty of dry climates and natural sources of ignition like lightning and volcanoes. At first the big summer fire across the mountain was blamed on a lightning strike and they do cause fires, but overall the most common trigger is human activity from agriculture, sparks from equipment, power lines arcing out, carelessness like a discarded cigarette-butt, and arson. This summer's fire is extraordinary however, and it's looking as if climate change is the overarching reason it is so catastrophic here and across the whole of the earth.

I begin to unpack our kit from the truck – their beds, food and water. There's no water running down the hill from our supply, so a careful regime for a while. I give them a drink, boil a kettle for some tea and take it out onto the terrace where I used to sit in the stillness listening out for the warblers and the noises of the forest. I wonder about the podengo who visited, his little short-legged friend and other dogs who roam through these woods, all the creatures who lived here, the deer and the boar, the beetles and my other guests who came to the butterfly ball.

I'm going down the track to see Carlos – he must have survived – and as I get nearer to his house I can see him and his family standing outside. No one speaks, and his wife just comes up and hugs me. After she lets go I walk over to Carlos, who has tears in his eyes, and I feel I'm welling up too. I ask him about the goats, and he says they survived, all of them. Has he got food? He says he has, but I note to bring them something later, to mark we are all okay. Making my way back up the track I think about water and a spring near Lucy's old house that should still be fine. Underground streams in these hills were the source of water for the hamlet; people washed their clothes

46

at the spring and there's still a place to do that. It's tough living though, especially in the winter months. We have enough food and the five litres from water man, so it's alright for now. There's ash everywhere; the house is covered and as soon as I clean it up there'll be more. I'm going to rest for a few hours and then do some yoga.

I start after brushing the terrace to get rid of the ash: clearing the space is important, the brushing is practical and symbolic. The best way to find our ground again through postures is to take our awareness to the feet in Tadasana, Mountain posture, and join the movement with the breath, which opens our energy body. The breath comes in through the nostrils, continues down through the chest so the whole rib cage opens gently, our bellies soften, we lengthen the spine and continue with this lengthening on the exhalation.

It's possible to join with the breath in this posture and focus on a single point. We guide the breath towards the navel and base of the spine, our point of focus, the seat of swadhisana and muladara chakra. As we exhale, keeping the point of concentration and lengthening the spine, the way begins to clear for the next inhalation and after a few breaths it allows a natural movement towards the next posture and our practice can flow as we move from the inside.

In *The Yoga Sutras* the limbs of yama and niyama, which deal with the ethical code of yoga, come before asana and pranayama because they provide the framework for our lives and practice. Hatha yoga is sometimes viewed differently in that it begins with the cleansing practices before moving on to asanas and pranayama, but the same ethics are also fundamental and risk being forgotten with the current emphasis on solely on postures, now that yoga is practised in gyms and so on throughout the world. It's crucial to remember that the concept of Hatha yoga is the conversion of matter, our physical body, into energy, to different conscious states that we can experience. The cells in our bodies change through practice, opening doors, and the ultimate goal of Hatha is the state of Yoga. This equates to samadhi in the sutras, the unity of Atman with Brahman in the Bhagavad Gita and unity with Spirit in the Upanishads. Hatha yoga is a pathway with such wide-reaching physical and mental benefits, helping us in so many ways, that this fundamental and overarching aspect risks being forgotten.

Fire, agni, igniting around the swadhisthana chakra in the vicinity of our bellies, is connected to the flow and release of the kundalini energy. This energy is most often represented visually by a snake coiled three and a half times around the spine in the classic image for muladara. The kundalini energy is usually viewed symbolically as the snake transforming and rising up the pathway of the energy channels of the nadis ida and pingala, which thread around the central susumna, all meeting up at various intersections, so to speak: the chakras.

The *Yoga Yajnavalkya* says specifically that the snake needs to be burned to achieve the transformation, that agni is introduced through pranayama and focus, dharana. It says that when she, the kundalini, is burned she wakes up and allows the prana to reach the base of the navel and rise up. Fundamentally it is all about energy and how we can transform one state into another, an alchemical process where matter is our physical body and the gold is pure energy, the essence of the universe. In our culture generally we see the serpent as evil, but this is based on some misunderstanding – Buddha is often depicted sitting on a nest of serpent gods with a massive hooded cobra over his head. Here the snake, often maligned, is a benign power in the universe and on earth.

There's no sound, the wind from the hurricane has finally dropped, no birds remain, no dogs are barking, everything is still. We're alone up here in this tiny hamlet in the forest, out of the village and the little town. Apart from Carlos, there were only two other neighbours living here: a friendly couple in a house that backs directly onto the forest. He's a surfer and was on the coast when the fire began to get hold. He got back in time and they evacuated just before me.

News is filtering through. There are going to be three days of national mourning – more than forty people have died so far – and a state of emergency has been declared in half the country's landmass. It's the worst fire for years; this one is part of hundreds of fires covering huge

48

swathes of the country. The state of emergency feels irrelevant and too late.

The Yoga Sutras creates a map to help us deal with hardship and suffering, which it calls dukkha. Dukkha is also present in the Upanishads, where the seers in the forest looked deeply into why there is dukkha manifesting as pain, death and ageing and ways in which we might cope. Dukkha is also the first of the four noble truths of the Buddha and fundamental to Hinduism as well as yoga, predating Buddhism in Indian ascetic tradition. It was Buddha, though, who helpfully put it into three categories of firstly physical suffering and pain, secondly of the stress and anxiety we experience in trying to hold things together in a world which is constantly changing, and thirdly the kind of malaise that the French writers Albert Camus and Jean-Paul Sartre expressed so well: a form of deep unease and alienation. At different times in our lives most of us experience some or all of these 'symptoms'. I know I have, and when they are felt acutely and chronically we become unwell.

For thousands of years, with a few exceptions, we've tried to resolve dukkha by directing our intelligence outwards to the physical world we inhabit. This made a lot of sense, it still does, and there's been extraordinary progress in so many ways but, as we all know, it has also given us more ingenious ways to destroy ourselves and our planet. We need a seismic shift in consciousness and it's not impossible that, if enough of us can change, this shift will happen. It's an old drum to beat, but we have to begin with ourselves.

It's going to be a long road back. I mean here in Cha with nature and how to live again. Eucalyptus trees like fires because their seeds survive even when the fire destroys the adult trees. The seeds use the ash as nutrition and they will soon spring up again so that in a couple of years there'll be even more. This fire will have destroyed the litter of the forest floors, reducing the chance of another major fire for a few years, but it will all build up again.

For now I need to begin by clearing the ash and finding some water. I try the tap again and this time some water comes out, brown and dense, but it will do to clean and I go to fetch a bucket. By the time I get back with it the water has stopped. I carry on sweeping, cleaning the ash and spend a little time sitting with the dogs.

A dog called Buddha

In the middle of the night Fox and Jimbo began barking and growling, jumping up at the window that looks over the big terrace. I couldn't see anything, no humans, boar, cats, rats or other creatures to get them this excited, and I tried to sleep again. They began again just as I was sinking back into sleep and this time I saw a huge dog running along the top of the wall; he turned as he sensed I'd seen him then jumped off and ran away. They barked on and off a few more times until dawn, when the thin yellow light of morning was filtering through the trees onto the terrace. I looked out again but still couldn't see anything. I put a pan of water on to boil some water for tea while I went outside to look. There was nothing there. The tea was invigorating; we were restless so I fed the dogs, did a practice and then we went up into the hills.

We walked in a big circle around Cha beneath a veil of cloud and smoke, small flames were still coming up from holes where trees or shrubs had been. I wondered about mudslides. It was, after all, October and the rain should already have started. It was a difficult walk with death in the air, a pyre of smoke and the familiar bitter smell that would linger for months.

Later in the day I saw the dog again. He was back running along the wall and the track next to it. I thought of the podengo and his little friend and that sometimes dogs just run through these woods then disappear. This one looked very thin, his yellow coat was covered in black ash and he looked as if he needed food and water. I took some outside and tried to get him to approach, tricky because Fox and Jim were barking all the time, but he did come eventually, drank lots of water and ate some food. He was a big dog with a head like a bear. He had no collar, was wary, but also wanted to come in which was difficult because by now even Weasel was barking at him from behind the closed door. They act as a pack and might attack this lovely bear-like creature because he was now on their turf.

I'm letting him in and keeping the others inside the house. As I close the gate to give him the run of the garden he goes straight up onto the terrace and stretches out on a sofa. I go to him and we like each other but the other dogs can see me sitting here through the long window onto the terrace and they're making a racket. Lucy has joined in too.

Time for a chat, which begins with a kind of dogs' 1970s-style encounter group on the floor all together. It's a fight and bite group; Jimbo has my arm in his huge jaws but knows we're playing, then it settles after a while into a transmission of togetherness and sitting quietly. They struggle with this last bit because the bear dog is on their terrace, but usually if they know I accept a dog they go through their stuff until eventually everyone accepts each other - it's a little different every time and so unpredictable. When Jimbo arrived, Fox hated him and still doesn't like him sitting too close, although Fox is quaint around his affections with other dogs, snappy one minute and cuddling up the next.

I go out onto the terrace and leave the door open, walk over to the bear dog and stroke him, followed by Fox, Weasel and Jimbo. Lucy stays inside. Weasel is fine, this new one is okay by me, but Fox and Jim don't want to know. It would take a little time to integrate another dog into this pack, and I need to find out if he has a home and if it is still there – unlikely from the state he's in – but much as I like him I have enough to manage for now.

Elsa

My neighbour up the track, the friendly surfer, saw the bear dog too and thought he might belong to a house down in the valley. He reminded me where the house was and shortly afterwards I got the dog in my truck, very easily as he was obviously used to vehicles, and we went down to see if he belonged there. I remembered I'd met one of the people who lived there before, decent enough folk. It wasn't their dog, but they thought they knew who might own it and left a text message for her. I took the bear dog back to Cha and, after a long drink, he settled himself down again on the sofa. He liked it there and I could see he would fit right in, sitting up on the yoga terrace surveying the valley below like his kingdom. It suited him but I needed to find his owner.

She appeared at the back entrance to the house a day later, after the message got through. I liked her energy: she was open and smiled like a child. She seemed pleased to meet me and was surprised we hadn't met before since we'd both been around for some time. She was German and had lived across the river for years. I asked the name of her dog.

"Buddha," she said, pronouncing it Boodha.

What sort of person calls their dog Buddha? I asked her in to have some tea.

Elsa's story is long, but the part around the fire was short. She lost everything. Her house burned along with all her stuff and she was still very traumatised.

From the yogic point of view, trauma and suffering is also in our physical and energy bodies; good therapists when working at a deeper level take this into account, to embrace what was going on for us in the womb for example. We are a work in progress after all, carrying not only the suffering of our own journey but also that of humanity. It's tough, and all we can do as individuals is try to shed some light on ourselves, on who we really are and what we're doing down here. It's an inner journey and most of the time we don't want to take a deep look into ourselves, the niyama swadiyaya in yoga. Yoga is a good way in because we can begin with our bodies, which will bring something up at some point anyway. Elsa didn't need this; she was already right in it. We had some tea and I listened for a long time, often the most helpful thing we can do for each other. Later I shared some postures and yoga nidra with her, which she said was a big help.

Part of yoga is the development of a witness consciousness in our minds that opens a way for us to move from identifying with form and the outer to an exploration, knowledge and better understanding of who we are. On one level this means we try to notice what is going on without attaching our ego to it, and we can begin to do it in our daily lives so knee jerk reactions decrease, reducing our stress. In yoga it's a part of practice. In postures there's a lot going on for us and this process is inextricably tied to it: we need to feel into the asana from the inside out. We can continue with pranayama and meditation, to develop this witness consciousness.

The ego is called asmita and is one of the main causes of our not seeing clearly. Not seeing clearly is avidhya and apart from ego is made up of three other parts: abinivesa which is fear, dvesa, a kind of wilful stubbornness, and raga, reaching and grabbing – desire might be a nicer way of putting this. We are caught between the horns of fear and desire, or greed in its extreme form, two polarities that have been prime movers in causing all wars and our present predicament. In ourselves, though, the four obstacles are an opportunity to take stock of where we stand in relation to them at any given moment. Eckert Tolle puts a lot down to the ego, to asmita, and with good reason. Culturally we suffer from avidhya in an extreme way, in part because of the domination in our culture by all things external, but it doesn't mean we can't progress: we definitely can.

Elsa told me Buddha's mother was a Tibetan mountain dog, a breed of guard dog used by nomadic tribes, villages and monasteries. His father was a husky, so he is actually smaller than the mountain dog but his bear-like head is more accentuated. She took him back and we agreed to meet up a week or so later to do some more yoga.

The next day

Amanha e um outro dia, tomorrow is another day, is often said over here. The dogs and I slept in the big room together again, all unsettled. Dogs like routine, and we've started early with a walk up through the hills around Cha, which we always do. Fox is showing a keen interest in the fire holes, his whole face is blackened already, and as I turn to check on the others I see he's vanished when I straighten back round. A few seconds, no sound or vision, he disappears like an apparition. I whistle and wait with about a seventy per cent chance of him coming straight back and if he doesn't do that he might turn up somewhere else as we walk on, or manifest, as if out of the ether, next to me. If he doesn't do either of those he might eventually come back to the house. Or not.

He has disappeared for a long time before, finally turning up ragged and thin, in bad shape. A few years ago he nearly lost his life in the woods, where he met up with some processionary caterpillars. The hairs on their bodies sting causing extreme allergic reactions to humans and they can be lethal to dogs who tend to be curious; they lick them so the hairs get embedded in the tongue which causes necrosis and death. Fox is nosey and must have come across some caterpillars and done that, licked one or tried to eat it. He came back one day with his tongue swollen, he was shaking and had difficulty breathing, his eyes were sunken, black and anxious. The vets in the nearest town know him and sent an ambulance over, he was treated with intravenous antihistamine, cortisone and taken in where he was on a drip overnight. Expected to lose some or all of his tongue, his chances of survival were on the low side, but somehow he made a full recovery. That was a good day.

I don't want to lose him now up here in this wilderness of ash and fire holes, and I keep whistling but walk on slowly. This is the best way with him, he anticipates the walk and might well be ahead somewhere anyway.

The cloud is all around us now: a thin, dark silver thread weaving ghostly shapes between the eucalyptus and covering the black skeletons of the burnt out pine. There is no sound, no songbirds or distant crows, no screech of a buzzard circling, nothing, nada. Then Fox appears out of the shadows with a large bone that's charred and blackened, poking out from the side of his jaws. He's pleased with himself. It's natural for him to dig around the corpses of the boar and other creatures who have died, but I get the bone off him. It all feels too recent; I know the animal's spirit has left and I'm interfering but I'm allowing myself to walk between the worlds. We carry on the path up the foothill and can see for miles. It's black everywhere, the fire didn't miss much, although some small random green patches are visible on the hill just below the horizon and distant buildings stand out like sugar lumps on coal. The cloud is thinner up here, it likes to hang around down in the valleys, and when the heather was out it reminded me of the glens in the Scottish Highlands. A long time ago, the heather, the Highlands, the axe-swinging warriors of my forebears...

I've tripped on a rock. I took my eyes off the track to look for Jimbo, who'd gone off into the shadows. These rescue dogs are more difficult to hold together because they've been completely feral. It takes time and patience, they follow their noses as all around them explodes into life, any sign of a deer or boar sets them on the trail, which is always up into the hills and away from where we are. I worry about their return journey if they end up on a road somewhere; they have at times and I've had to scoop them up in the truck.

We've moved on and I can hear Jimbo behind us running very fast. He'll gallop past tight to my legs and I bend my knees in anticipation in case he misjudges it. He's still very young and his need for speed hasn't been curbed by a nasty wound from a metal statue of Shiva that ripped his leg as he dashed past it. A lot of stitches. I did something similar once, a long time ago, when I was a boy scrumping apples and got caught by the farmer. I ran, climbed up into a hay loft and was trapped so jumped down twelve feet or so, landing on a metal spike not unlike the one on the Shiva statue that Jim ran into. I had a lot of stitches too and we both have the scar.

We're all back together in the cloud, which is more like early morning fog, and the sky is hanging like a slate roof above us and feeling as if it could collapse. I'm breathing hard: it's a steep climb up to the top of the hill and a path that runs along the ridge.

Up above the cloud now the path has joined a track that I know runs for miles deep into a cork forest before eventually joining the road that twists back round to Cha. We change direction off the track and head back down into the haze of the cloud. It feels like a dream that's blurred and vague before it comes into sharp relief and the part that can wake us up.

Jimbo and Fox are on leads now; I'm tired and don't want to trek back up hills looking for them. They usually behave well and accept the arrangement, at least until they come across anyone, or other dogs, when they act out very badly, pulling and straining on the leash, Fox with hackles up and both barking. Out here though it's a rarity to come across anyone.

The descent is going well; I'm picking my way and reflective. We are nature, as much as the birds, the boar, the deer, all the creatures, and when part of the natural world has suddenly gone from around us it reverberates within us on a cellular level. I can't even see a single spider's web left to reflect what light there is; before at this time of year they spun perfection when they hung like miniature rainbows in the morning sun. Death, in the form of the grim reaper, has struck in this forest and there were no niceties like the conversation with Nachiketas.

Shapes come and go in this mist, drifting in and out of my vision, a bit lighter now as we walk down through a clearer patch, and I'm remembering a time, years ago, in the Highlands of Scotland.

There was a hill, a Munro, close to where I was staying and easy to walk to. I'd been up a few hills before, the weather was fine, and I felt like a gentle climb so set off, forgetting to tell anyone where I was going. Over here I often don't see another human all day, sometimes for two or three days, and rely on myself, usually going up in the hills without a mobile or much else. I did the same in Scotland but it's more foolish to do it there, where the weather can change fast, conditions are different and generally much harsher. It was spring and the weather very changeable but the sun on the hillside and the ferns swaying gently in the breeze got me up and out without thinking of much else.

I got to the top well enough although it was more of a climb than I'd expected. It was steeper and cold too; an icy wind probed my jacket and a mist began to mushroom along the narrow ridge as I made my way. I had to grip the rocks with both hands and clamber slowly, which took a long while, and when it should have begun to descend it opened out like a field, although the mist was so thick by now I couldn't see where it ended. It was covered with dense springy grass and moss, the kind you get on the moors where you can also sink in quickly, and I could only see a few feet in front by now. I thought of my crommach, the long walking stick used in the Highlands for all sorts of things – checking out the ground in front was one of them. Mine was a gift from the gillie, crafted over long winter nights, and I remembered his words clearly as I pictured it in my mind's eye nestled up by the back door with the rest of my kit: "You'll be needing this!"

I carried on walking and trying to find the edge of the little plateau. It was silly; I couldn't see much, was losing my sense of direction, and thought I'd better try to find some shelter and wait it out for a while to see if the mist lifted.

A frog caught my attention as I sat crouching in the shelter of a hollow in an outcrop of rocks. We were staring at each other, millions of evolutionary years between us but I felt a mutual sense of disbelief, I shouldn't have been there and I wasn't sure what he was doing there either, although he probably had some family around somewhere. I was pleased to see him though and we sat there for a while together but it was getting colder as the time passed and I decided to have one more go at finding my way off the hill. I said goodbye to my friend and began walking in what I hoped was a straight line that sooner or later would get me off the plateau. I couldn't really be sure but it was so cold I didn't want to be still and decided to walk on until I either began to descend somewhere or was just too tired to keep going. If that happened I'd find the best place I could to wait it out until daybreak. That was the sensible thing to do anyway; stumbling into a bog could lead to any number of problems but I chanced it and walked on. After time the ground changed, there were small rocks that I tripped on once or twice but it felt firmer beneath my feet and my fear of a bog got less. I wasn't tired yet; I was fixated on getting back down and kept going.

Here in the hills behind Cha we're nearly back at the house. The cloud has gone but is hanging low down in the valley, a still white cloak shrouding the darkness beneath it.

Water: the future of our planet and humanity depends on it. I muse as I watch a trickle from the kitchen tap, still thick and brown, it splutters and dies then surprises me by coming back again. I leave the tap open, a little more trickles through which I quickly catch in a bowl before it stops and then boil some of the other water in a pan on the gas for tea. We're back home and the dogs, except Lucy, are telling me that they think this whole fire thing is no good at all: after being crammed and cramped in the truck for days, nothing is going on, it's black and cold, no decent scents, no random noises to bark at, no neighbours to annoy, nothing, nada, and somewhere in the mix it's my fault. But it's just a moment, then they have a drink and work out who's going to lie down where and relax. The water begins trickling through again, clearer now, and I grab the kettle and fill it, then root around for the other containers to fill them and get two buckets as well. Then it stops, the tap's open but that's it, no more. I close the tap and get my mat out to begin a practice.

You don't always need a mat to do yoga postures. It's good to do some standing asanas, or all of them in your practice, where your feet can connect directly to the earth. If bare feet on the earth isn't possible it's fine, it all still happens when you consciously connect to your feet. You don't need special clothes either, you can do standing postures anywhere that you can stand up with a bit of room to move your legs. Obvious, but useful if for example you're driving a long distance and need to carry on. Stop somewhere and do fifteen minutes of standing asanas; it gives enough good clear energy for a few more hours and is one way of bringing a part of your practice into your daily life.

Up in the Highlands the mist had changed, becoming thin and grey. There were bigger patches where it was completely clear, I could see yards in front of me, and if it carried on sooner or later I'd get a fix on where I was. It felt much better, gave me some more energy. I was flagging, but now I could see the sky in some clear patches and was out of the dark. Not quite into the light though; that took a few more hours picking my way over or around rock outcrops and marshy grassland to a steep descent the other side of the mountain. I'd come a long way, ending up on a track I recognized in the pine forest near the house, and I eventually made my way in through the back door, past my crommach and my backpack with kit inside and its little stove for brewing tea. I suppose it takes some people a long time to learn a simple lesson.

One miracle at a time, one day at a time. I was thinking again about our situation here back in Cha and that thought came up, to piece together a way forward, and sometimes it's all we can do, start from where we are and be clear about our intention. Alignment plays a part in this and, from the yogic perspective, another reason why postures can be so helpful but we need balance and if we only focus on the outer form, so that it becomes more important than the inner attunement, we lose our way. Postures aren't just physical and when we allow the inhalation or exhalation to guide us from the inside out it's the beginning of a lot of positive changes. We want our bodies to be strong but not held or pushed or pulled, so our energy is flowing and moving like nature itself, like a wave on the ocean. This is what the Upanishads are about as much as anything, an experiential tuning in to nature, and why they are full of natural imagery.

The rest of the day passed around more clearing up because there was water and this time enough to wash some clothes. We went for a short walk, ate, and as dusk fell I lit some candles before sitting for a while then sleeping with the dogs in the big room. Lucy had the bed close by me and she'd quietened down more at night but sometimes she still woke up disturbed. As she was close I could put a hand on her, which calmed her down, other times I got out of bed to hold her and eventually we'd all get back to sleep.

More news is coming through this morning. The fires have raged across the north and central regions, killing forty-one people so far with a lot of serious injuries. Firefighting and rescue services have been overwhelmed and unable to cope. Around 500,000 hectares have burnt and as one survivor has been quoted as saying, "It felt like the end of the world."

It's raining now. We need the rain but I'm still remembering the mudslides from before. It depends on the intensity of the rain, how long it lasts, so we need to wait and see.

Chapter Five

The rain came and went. Some days were clear and sunny, on others the rain didn't stop. The friendly surfer up the track left, they had no electricity or solar panels then and it was taking months to get people reconnected. We were alone in the tiny hamlet, the days were getting colder and part of them was spent fetching wood to keep our stove alight. Fires like space, somewhere to go, a future with fuel, and I chopped logs into thin strips to get them going in the mornings then into some thicker bits until the big ones went on. When it was really cold I did a practice inside and close to the flames, agni.

No two practices are the same. Even if we sequence the postures in exactly the same way, same breath patterns and so on, the experience will always be slightly different and we'll always finish in a different place to the one we started in. We need to adapt our practice to our needs and develop a good understanding of each posture and its purpose. In those cold mornings I often started with a more dynamic approach and as the asanas warmed me up it was more comfortable to move through the sequence to sit. In sitting postures we need to give ourselves to the earth.

As autumn passed Lucy became very settled into the routine and we spent a lot of time together in a different way to the others because she needed help to get around. Although she'd got stronger, and was looking well with her shiny coat and bright eyes, she couldn't manage steps; we did them together and it meant I needed to be around all of the time. I thought what an incredible companion she would have been if we'd met when she could walk and run, but as our time together grew we developed an understanding that moved into a different space, where our thoughts and hearts met in a silent place.

61

In the winter that followed it rained and rained. We spent our time trying to stay warm and on morning walks, if the cloud wasn't low, I could see the small trails of smoke that curled from the chimneys of the white houses in the valley below: everyone was doing the same. It was hard to find anything green to bring into the house, to remind us of the change the solstice was bringing and that spring would arrive, but the light began to change and the thin sun felt a little warmer on my back. As the days grew longer a few green shoots appeared in the forest, but it was slow and a long way from other years in February, when I'd wake to the songbirds at dawn. It was a silent spring.

That silent spring became a long hot summer. Every Sunday the sirens sounded, the dogs howled, we kept an eye each day for news of fires or any long trails of smoke spreading across the sky. The big fires came, but this time in the south. The ones up here were smaller and more controllable. Temperatures rocketed to forty-six degrees centigrade in parts of the country; we were fairly constant in the high thirties and low forties on some days. The rest of the continent was melting too. Greece suffered really badly, had the same three days of national mourning, state of emergency and death toll north of a hundred.

We still lived one day at a time, getting up early and getting things done before the heat made it difficult. Nature was slowly recovering. Some cicadas came back and butterflies appeared: swallowtails, fritillaries, holly blues. There was the scent of rosemary again. In the garden fruit trees began to ripen and in July the small green figs swelled as wasps gathered for sanctuary among the broad leaves. The sunsets were yellow and gold, their light spread in sheets across the terraces as I sat waiting for dusk and that crack between the worlds which opens just enough for our spirits to find a way to the stars.

So that summer passed and as another autumn began to feel its way a nightjar graced us with evening flights around the terrace and across the open spaces above the house. I sat in stillness as it passed like a disappearing soul into the night. Then one evening it didn't show, nor the next and it never came back; I waited but it was gone.

One day melted into another, and I lost count of the ones I didn't see another human. My life had changed. It was Lucy. Unconditional love had filled the silent space between us.

We kept warm and walked every day. Lucy always started first and we followed her until she stopped and I carried her back home. She couldn't go far but she always came and it was a daily celebration of freedom for all of us.

One early morning a hen harrier perched on the terrace and I froze to complete stillness, gazing at this extraordinary creature. We should be just as thrilled to see a robin or a sparrow, the human obsession with the exotic in nature hasn't always served us well, but it was impossible not to stop in amazement at this wonderful hawk as she sat motionless, fully alive and in the moment. I learned that the females are distinct from the males, who tend to be almost pale grey in colour: the females are brown with a clear white ring on the tail feathers. Why would anyone kill these magnificent creatures, drive them almost to extinction? She spent a few weeks with us and I got to know where she liked to sit, which trees and time of day. Jim didn't like her and barked when she was near so I kept him in by the fire in the mornings and at dusk, when she often appeared, although she also liked the afternoons, settling on a tall burnt out pine that was a long time dead, one I'd been meaning to fell and burn. Then she left, like the nightjar. I waited for her but she'd gone.

Fox and Jim vanished one day. I waited and searched for a long time, hours, and then went back up in the truck to see if they were around. It was wet and muddy, rough going with burnt eucalyptus trunks jammed across the track. I had to move them before following it to finally join up with the road that the dogs could have reached.

I drove along it slowly and, as I turned a bend, a herd of deer ran straight across in front of me so that I had to brake very hard to avoid hitting them, thinking it was fortunate for them I was driving slowly and looking for the dogs. Were they chasing them? The deer stopped just across the road from me and close by; the leader was staring at me and I thought they were waiting for a straggler. As I looked into her eyes she was making it very clear I needed to go so I crept on, curious to see if any more crossed the road after I'd gone. None did, the herd remained very still and weren't joined by any others. Then after a few minutes they turned round and ran off up into the hills. I waited there, perhaps the dogs were on their trail but still some way behind, but they didn't appear and as the thin sun was beginning to sink behind the trees and the light was fading I headed back, hoping they might be there.

There was still no sign of them though as I made a fire and reminded myself that Fox was cunning and worldly, that he had done this plenty of times before. It was Jim who worried me; he could run so fast following his nose with no sense of anything else in his path, like the statue of Shiva. He was still very young. Once before he had run off with Fox and I'd scooped him up as he spun at full speed round a blind corner almost into my truck. Fox was close behind him and stared at me with a, 'you're not supposed to be here,' look as I grabbed him too: tricky as he has an ability to shrink his neck and slip his collar. He did it memorably in the UK, one of many times before I finally realized he would never fit in there.

We were in a rural hamlet in Devon, open country more or less, and Fox had taken himself off and got in the middle of a pack of hounds and the hunt. It was mayhem and as I went to catch him he slipped his collar and ran off, barking and snarling at the hounds, looking more like a fox than a fox. I couldn't get hold of him, and then Weasel and Jim joined in as they'd heard the kerfuffle. Horses were spooking, the riders were confused by this podengo with his Spock-like ears and so I asked them to ride on, just go, and I'd deal with the swirling chaos of Fox and the hounds. He was still snarling and barking as Weasel ran in circles around all of them, confusing Jim who stood like a gypsy's lurcher in the middle of them all. The hounds had quickly got that Fox was actually a dog, it was the humans who'd been confused and it all calmed down as they moved on so I managed to get hold of Fox. Jim and Weasel did what they were told and followed me back. The master of the hounds was my neighbour; he lived across a couple of fields and knew I could ride a bit but was very anti-hunting. Lucy beckoned from afar.

Through the terrace window I could see the first stars appearing above us in the southern sky when I heard a noise outside, a rustling that was loud enough to be of interest, and I got up from lying by the fire with Weasel and Lucy to see what it was. Jim was standing just outside the gate, wet, mud soaked and panting. A huge relief; Fox could take care of himself but this one had a lot to learn. I got him in and he went straight to the water bowl, drinking half of it at once. Good. Fox might be close as well; they'd often come back more or less together when they'd run off for a shorter time so it was on the cards. I went to get something to rub Jim down with and on my way Fox appeared at the door, contrite and wagging his tail. He was black with mud and ash that was still on the cork trees even now, and he followed Jim to the water bowl. I did what I always do when they've run off; I rewarded bad behaviour and gave them a meal, which they wolfed down. Always celebrate the return of the prodigal; one day they may not be there.

The space between Lucy and I had developed to include a deep recognition. I'd catch her looking at me when I was minding my own business, ask her silently if she needed something, was she alright and so on but began to realize her gaze wasn't about that. Years ago I'd read the *Anam Cara* by the Irish author John O'Donohue, with its concept of soul recognition, and it dawned on me that I was experiencing this with Lucy. We had found a place where we connected to somewhere other.

That winter brought a plague of mice: the fire had played havoc with their natural predators, owls, buzzards and so on. I couldn't find any traps for sale here that didn't kill them, and spent a lot of evenings catching them under a frying pan propped up in the sink. They'd go down there to eat the bits of food I left for them, pretty well anything, and I left a window half open so I could see their reflections in the black glass as they ran along the worktop and down into the sink. Then I went in quickly and caught them in a tea towel, put them in a box and took them a long way off into the forest. I managed to catch about fifty. They were clever and fast and there were more but, as the warmer weather came in the spring, they moved outside anyway. I could see them once in a while, running around in the grass under the trees.

The following summer was fine and more normal. We were spared from any big fires here but around the country there were more than the year before and it was still a big problem. We lived each day fully, getting up early in the cool of the morning and up into the hills. There was a rhythm to the days that joined with the cicadas' into the evenings, when we sat out on the terrace after the sun had set and the moon was up.

Lucy wanted to spend all her time with me and was close by my side unless I was out, which was only ever briefly and measured because of her. I wanted to be with her too and make sure she was alright, to move her to a cool spot if it looked as if she needed it.

Just after the solstice she found everything more difficult, it was hot and there are some days here, when the temperature's up, it's an effort to do much at all. I thought at first it was the heat but it became clear her body wasn't working as it had been, struggling even in the cool of the morning to walk down the gentle slope of the track which she loved and had been managing so well. We went to the vets, who could find nothing specifically wrong with her and I took her back home relieved but unsettled. I felt her time here and our time together was drawing to a close. We just carried on; I picked her up whenever I saw she needed it but I must have missed times when she did. As a few more weeks passed her body began to let her down more and more.

Her spirit was the same – her eyes shone like stars and we were the same together, the same connection – but I knew we'd have to let go. I was carrying her more or less everywhere, she couldn't get up much, and we'd look at each other both knowing we were up the final creek without a paddle.

Some years after my time in Africa I met a highly regarded Celtic shaman. At our first meeting, with no knowledge of where I'd been, she quizzed me about my time there, and it led us to agree I should learn the craft from her. Over about three years she taught me, transmitting a great deal, and as our work together was drawing to a close, when I was going to see her less frequently, I heard she'd gone into hospital where she died after a very short time. She had told me more than once she felt uncomfortable in her body, but her passing like this was a shock and caused me huge pain and grief. Shamanic journeys confirmed for me that her soul needed to leave her body because it was worn out.

Now it's Lucy, she's in the same boat. I'd taken her on and I'm responsible for her; it's what we should do for beings who aren't human but who share their time here on Earth with us, many of whom we've domesticated like donkeys, horses, goats, sheep, and cows. There's no difference between a cow's feelings for its offspring and any other mammal's, so taking its baby away so we can drink its milk is something we shouldn't be doing, especially on an industrial scale. One thing is for sure: we shouldn't eat them. Our continued abuse of animals is a direct reflection of our own lack of progress but we can change, we're not stuck in gear.

I undertook a journey for Lucy and me to try and get an answer about whether we should be looking at euthanasia, something I wanted to avoid although I didn't want her to suffer. I journeyed after she couldn't stand up even long enough to have a cool drink, when I had to hold her. The journey made it crystal clear to me that her soul was ready to leave and I needed to midwife its passage to save her physical body torment, she had had enough of that in her life.

I called her vet, Estela, a deeply empathetic spirit who had seen Lucy from day one when I rescued her. Since then I'd shown her some yoga and we'd become friends. It was the morning, and we agreed to meet in the house later on towards the evening.

I cleaned everywhere, prepared incense, candles and a place for Lucy's body which I'd planned to bury under an olive at the front of the house. We spent time together, I lay down beside her a while and then she transmitted quite clearly she didn't want her body to be buried here, she wanted to be cremated. At the same time as hearing the words I had a vision of a funeral pyre and a white cloth.

Estela arrived and we sat on the floor by Lucy, who was lying down on the bed I'd prepared with a clean white cotton sheet on top of it. I shut the others outside after they'd greeted Estela and she lit more candles, put a circle of some small stones that had special significance for her around Lucy and then we sat quietly together. After a little while Estela anaesthetized her and I chanted the Gayatri mantra as Lucy drifted off, then Estela administered the final injection. I'm not ashamed to say I cried a river.

Although well into the evening, the sun hadn't gone down and splinters of golden light fell onto the floor where we sat for a while before Estela left and Lucy and I were alone. I let the others back in. They knew she'd gone and were very subdued while we sat together quietly.

Later on I moved to a chair and carried on sitting with her after the sun had set and it was dark. It felt time to have music, good for our spirits, and I thought of my favourite raga from Ravi Shankar, *Raga Bairagi*, which I've sometimes put on for a practice, deliberately breaking the no music with postures rule, because it reflects the light in nature, and so in us. Then I had a transmission from Lucy, like the one when she'd made it clear she wanted to be cremated, and now she was asking for Gregorian chants to be played. I didn't have any, nothing downloaded and hadn't played any for about a decade. I tinkered with my phone, eventually found some and sat with her listening to the monks singing *Agnus Dei* and other chants, deep into the night.

Bardo is a transitional state and revealed especially in *The Tibetan Book of the Dead*, a book for living as much as dying. Death is the fourth bardo and an opportunity to join with the luminous essence of all that is and to be liberated from samsara, the karmic wheel of birth and death. The book itself is layered, complex and steeped in frames of reference and knowledge which are a lifetime's work, or many lifetimes work, to begin to embrace. For Lucy the Gregorian chants were significant. The Tibetans believe, and so do I, that although the body may no longer have life there is an energy which can hear and it's why the book is read in its entirety to those who are dying and dead. To me her request meant that her spirit was communicating from one of the non-physical realms, from the etheric. This energy exists but, at the time of writing anyway and as far as I know, we've yet to have the evidence-based proof that it is so. A dog has a spirit the same as we do.

Her body stayed peacefully on her bed and I journeyed again to see if she'd crossed the rainbow bridge – not the rainbow bridge that is circulated on the net, although that's a lovely idea with some similarities. There are forty-nine days in bardo which relate directly to the number seven, the number of main chakras whose colours are represented in the rainbow. These etheric colours also have representative sounds, seed sounds in yoga and used in yogic chants like the Gayatri mantra. Buddhist monk chants vibrate on these frequencies and so do some Gregorian chants.

I did a shamanic journey where my power animals confirmed Lucy's safe crossing into the light, but they told me not to communicate with her, something normally done through a power animal or guide. This disappointed me, somehow I'd assumed that we might be in touch in some way, which would help with the awful grief I was experiencing, but any message like this is sacrosanct and so I busied myself with the physical world. I made a cup of tea.

The others were miserable, their energy was low, there was a chasm left by Lucy for all of us and the next day we went out into the hills. Sometimes when I go out with them I stop if there's something of particular interest to them. They pick up a whole other world that speaks of trails and creatures who've passed by earlier, whole stories that lay quietly in a branch or on the earth, waiting to be read. Jim often stands motionless to my eyes, staring into the bush, and then quite often I can see how a branch or fern has been disturbed, that there's trail to follow.

I moved on. This walk was difficult, Lucy on my mind and in my soul; it was silent and empty in the hills as we made our way. Going downhill on a sandy bit of the track some butterflies appeared, not unusual but it was good to see these holly blues dancing around us, their wings luminescent in the morning sun. Then more joined in the dance, staying with us and around me as I walked, then even more, so many I stopped to hold their message close, deep in my heart.

In the evening of the next day I was watering a small rockery and garden I'd made for her. A dragonfly began to fly round me, one of the big ones. It stayed, close to her lemon tree and to me. A good moment. I finished watering the plants and went inside, more tea. I had to go out again though, so took the tea with me to see if the dragonfly was still around, and I went over to the lemon tree. It flew back, its wings reflecting all the colours of the rainbow in the evening sun.

About the Author

Steve Jamison is a yoga teacher, therapist and writer spending his time between central Portugal and South Devon. He began yoga in the 1970s and continued to practise daily as he travelled to, as he put it, "Find my way in the world." He spent some years surfing in Africa before returning to the UK to form a band in London and then his own clothing design company, one of the first to design and successfully sell vegan clothes, including a collection to Bloomingdales in New York. During this period he took up Kyushindo karate, which he subsequently taught. Steve returned to 'serious' yoga twenty years ago, spent ten years learning from Ranju Roy and Jenny Beeken, and began teaching. *A Dog Called Buddha* is his first book.

Blue Poppy Publishing

Founded in 2016, Blue Poppy is based in Ilfracombe, North Devon. It is not a traditional publisher, but instead assists local authors to self-publish their books while retaining overall control. At the same time, it is not a 'vanity' publisher, in that we take great care to publish books which are well written, properly edited, and have professional formatting and cover work.

Nevertheless, as a small publisher we rely heavily on word of mouth to promote our books. So, if you have enjoyed this book, please, please take a few moments to write a review. You can review books on our own website, www.bluepoppypublishing.co.uk, as well as on social media, and Goodreads. If you write for a blog that's even better. Please let us know if you post about it in a blog so that we can promote it.

You can also email us at info@bluepoppypublishing.co.uk